A VISUAL JOURNEY OF WARTIME PATRIOTISM

UNITED
WE STAND!

RICHARD J. PERRY

COLLECTORS PRESS

PORTLAND, OREGON

REFERENCES:
National Archives
Library of Congress
British Nutrition Foundation
The Women's Army Corps
The New York Times

Library of Congress Cataloging-in-Publication Data

Perry, Richard J.
United we stand! : a visual journey of wartime patriotism / by
Richard J. Perry.
    p. cm.
  ISBN 1-888054-64-6
1. World War, 1939–1945– United States– Pictorial works.
2. Patriotism– United States– Pictorial works.   I. Title.
D769 .P48 2002
940.53'73– dc21

                                              2001006679

INTERIOR DESIGN · *Trina Stahl*
EDITING · *Ann Granning Bennett*
FRONT COVER AND FLAPS · *Michael Graziolo,*
                            Drive Communications, NY
BACK COVER AND FLAPS · *Evan Holt*
FLAT PHOTOGRAPHY · *Fred Wilson*
3-D PHOTOGRAPHY · *Meredith Quarterman*

The cover image is men and women of the American Red
Cross taken in Paris, France at the end of World War II. The
newspaper headlines originally read "Peace."

Printed in Singapore
9 8 7 6 5 4 3 2 1

Collectors Press books are available at special discounts
for bulk purchases, premiums, and promotions. Special
editions, including personalized inserts or covers, and
corporate logos, can be printed in quantity for special
purposes. For further information contact: Special Sales,
Collectors Press, Inc., P.O. Box 230986, Portland, OR 97281.
Toll-free: 1-800-423-1848

For a free catalog write: Collectors Press, Inc., P.O. Box
230986, Portland, OR 97281. Toll-free: 1-800-423-1848 or
visit our website at: www.collectorspress.com

This book is dedicated to the victims of terrorism worldwide

The Author would like to extend a special thanks to the following people:

Lisa Perry, my wife and partner, for her key research, suggestions, and unwavering support

My son Keaton and daughter Ava, my two shining stars, for reminding me every day what "united" means in our home front

Trina Stahl who worked an incredible schedule designing this book without a single complaint

Ann Bennett for her indispensable editorial guidance

Michael Graziolo, friend and colleague, who designed the front cover in record time

Evan Holt for his technical assistance

Lori Cunningham for her research

Margaret Johnson for her research ideas

Paul Vanderpool of The Raven Antiques in Sellwood, Oregon

John Gearhart who unselfishly supplied his time and collection, and his brother Mark Gearhart of Sellwood Antique Mall

★ ★

INTRODUCTION

★ ★

War has always underscored the meaning of patriotism.

The Declaration of Independence, America's symbol of freedom most eloquently expresses its essence: ". . . all men are created equal, that they are endowed by their Creator with certain unalienable Rights, that among these are Life, Liberty and the pursuit of Happiness." To understand this statement is to understand Americans, because from this core concept is American patriotism derived.

Perhaps no conflict is better remembered for the patriotism it inspired than World War II. In part, this is due to radio and mass printing, which enabled those on the home front to learn of the successes in battles of the United States and its allies. But, in all truth, Americans have always found a way to rally together for a cause.

The bombing of Pearl Harbor awakened an America still wounded from the Great Depression. The horrific event rallied the nation as no other event in history. Unemployment, at an estimated 25 percent, virtually vanished as thousand of men were drafted into the Armed Services. Left behind were job opportunities in fields such as machine and equipment work that the government

REMEMBER

V

PEARL HARBOR

★ ★ ★ ★ ★ ★ ★ ★ ★ ★ ★ ★ ★ ★ ★ ★ ★ ★

I'm Proud... my husband wants me to do my part

SEE YOUR U. S. EMPLOYMENT SERVICE
WAR MANPOWER COMMISSION

WAR WORKER

previously had restricted to male operators. Now the nation needed laborers, and the government reclassified more than one-half of all jobs to allow women and African-Americans to fill them.

At first, only single women came forth to accept these jobs. But by the time the United States completed its first all-American bombing raid on Germany in 1943, married women were allowed to work— and eventually they outnumbered single women in the workplace. By 1944, about one-third of the entire workforce were women. One out of every five women enlisted in the Army, often believing that if they helped win the war, they would get their fathers, husbands, and brothers home faster.

Advertising campaigns using posters and brochures, with copy promising good pay, proved successful recruiting devices. Many women stepped into their husbands' jobs, knowing it wouldn't be difficult to give them back once the men came home. But others, who enjoyed their newly gained financial independence, intended on keeping their jobs after the war.

The social unacceptability of women working, especially in jobs requiring physical labor, led to a good deal of backlash from men. Women were absent from work more than men, because they had children to take care of, and day care was in its infancy. These times produced "latchkey children," who—unsupervised—let themselves in and out of the house and also took care of their younger siblings.

Most men did not approve of women in the workplace, but women kept their spirits high, knowing in their hearts the

★ ★

WAAC MONTHLY PAY SCALE

OFFICERS:
Colonel $333.33
Lt. Colonel $291.67
Major $250.00
Captain $200.00
1st Lieutenant $166.67
2nd Lieutenant $150.00

ENROLLED MEMBERS:
Master Sergeant $138.00
First Sergeant $138.00
Technical Sergeant $114.00
Staff Sergeant $96.00
Technician, 3rd Grade $96.00
Sergeant $78.00
Technician, 4th Grade $78.00
Corporal $66.00
Technician, 5th Grade $66.00
Private, 1st Class $54.00
Private $50.00

To the ladies, God bless them!

HERE YOU SEE a force that Hitler and Tojo sadly underestimated—*American womanpower.*

Day and night, throughout the U.S. aircraft industry, women by the thousands are working to upset the Axis applecart. Women who were stenographers, home-bodies, salespeople . . . the girl next door . . .

They multiply mightily our productive power. Make it possible for ever-growing swarms of warplanes to roar off our production lines.

The airplanes built by Northrop men and women carry a message from free people — in the only words the enemy seems to understand. And even as our planes speak in enemy skies, the Northrop group works on — creating and building yet more deadly aircraft.

NORTHROP
Aircraft, Inc.

BUY WAR BONDS WITH ALL YOUR MIGHT BACK UP THE ARMY WHO FLY OUR PLANE

P AIRCRAFT, INC. · NORTHROP FIELD, HAWTHORNE, CALIFORNIA · MEMBER AIRCRAFT WAR PRODUCTION COUNCIL, INC.

1944 advertisement for Northrop Aircraft pays tribute to two Rosie the Riveters, who broke the mold of the stereotypical, homegrown "girl next door."

importance of their labor and their place in maintaining morale of the nation.

For women, the war brought unanticipated benefits. It gave them an opportunity to challenge male prejudice and the well-established social order. Stereotypes were broken as "Rosie the Riveter"—a term given to all women in the workplace, not just those who riveted aircraft—demonstrated her abilities in positions formerly held by men. They were welders, mechanics, factory workers, bus drivers, tractor operators, and mail deliverers; again the incentive was to get their men home safe, sound, and fast. Undoubtedly the most famous Rosie the Riveter was Norma Jean Baker, a pretty brunette discovered in an aircraft plant by a photographer for *Yank* magazine. Her picture was widely published and praised. She later changed her hair color to blond and her name to Marilyn Monroe.

Many women became nurses. When the United States entered World War II, the American Red Cross quickly responded by expanding its services to support the war effort. Out of outrage from the attack on Pearl Harbor, hospitals recruited nurses by the thousands; many women took on jobs as seamstresses and bandage wrappers to keep up with the demand for them in overseas battle zones. The Red Cross created a blood donation program, and discrimination in the hiring ranks finally came to an end—for the time being.

On February 4, 1941, under President Roosevelt's call for action, six civilian agencies grouped resources to form the United Service Organizations (U.S.O.) to organize and establish recreational facilities for soldiers and their families. Operated by volun-

THEY'RE DOING THEIR PART

"Tell us how we can help and we'll do it." That expresses the patriotic spirit of the average American—man or woman.

Pictured above is one group of loyal workers engaged in Red Cross activity. Union Pacific has formed many of these groups in the territory which it serves. And there are many similar organizations throughout the Nation.

The work of groups who prepare bandages is carefully supervised. Each bandage must be made to exacting specifications; the slightest speck of foreign matter must be removed.

These women are not "playing at war." They are cheerfully giving their time to perform a vital and painstaking task. They are doing their part and doing it well.

The Progressive

UNION PACIFIC RAILROAD

ROAD OF THE STREAMLINERS AND THE CHALLENGERS

This Union Pacific Railroad ad reads: "These women are not 'playing at war'. They are cheerfully giving their time . . . and doing it well."

teers, the clubs and hospitality houses offered live entertainment, dancing, and movies; places of solitude to write or to seek religious counseling; and the opportunity to just get a free cup of coffee and a dough-nut. They were located wherever possible—in storefronts, barns, muse-ums, railroad cars, churches, mu-seums, and yacht clubs. More than 3,000 such clubs flourished during World War II, hosting not just men, but also women in uniform and military wives in need of childcare.

U.S.O. clubs headlined both no-name and big-name entertainers. Among the latter group, perhaps none were more famous than Bob Hope, Bette Davis, and Marlene Dietrich, who took their shows on the road to hospitals and bases around the world, often coming close to enemy lines, to bring smiles to the faces of servicemen. Not all the entertainers made it home. Many were lost en route to battle zones or fell victim next to fighting men.

"Commando Mary" was the military counterpart to Rosie the

The Andrews Sisters (left to right, Maxine, Pattie, and LaVerne) performing for a packed audience of servicemen. Their hit wartime songs were "Boogie Woogie Bugle Boy" (1941), "I'll Be With You in Apple Blossom Time" (1941), and "Don't Sit Under the Apple Tree" (1942).

★ ★ ★ ★ ★ ★ ★ ★ ★ ★ ★ ★ ★ ★ ★ ★ ★ ★ ★ ★

★ ★ ★ ★ ★ ★ ★ ★ ★ ★ ★ ★ ★ ★ ★ ★ ★ ★ ★ ★

Riveter. Initially the public had difficulty accepting a woman in uniform, but eventually they realized that additional resources were badly needed in both industry and military and that women could offer special talents and abilities.

In 1941, the government accepted women into service and created the Women's Army Auxiliary Corps (WAACs). In 1943 the "Auxiliary" was dropped and The Women's Army Corps (WACs) was created, providing women with special training, rank, living quarters, and medical care. However, they were not allowed access to positions requiring them to command men, and they received less pay and fewer benefits than men.

Women also served in the Marine Corps Women's Reserve (MCWR), the Navy's WAVES, the Coast Guard's SPARs (an acronym based on the Coast Guard motto: "Semper Paratus— Always Ready"), the Army Nurse Corps (ANC), and Navy Nurse Corps (NNC). They also served in the Women's Air Force Service Pilots (WASP), a collective of various Air Force branches, in which they flew troops and supplies around the world.

By the end of the war, women were hailed for their contributions, and a crack in the door for an equal rights movement was officially made.

Automobile makers got into the act in 1942 by shifting production from traditional vehicles to armored cars, trucks, jeeps, anti-aircraft and anti-tank guns, and airplane engines. Chrysler alone produced more than 25,000 tanks in the United States during

★ ★ ★ ★ ★ ★ ★ ★ ★ ★ ★ ★ ★ ★ ★ ★ ★ ★ ★ ★

International Trucks hooked up with Brink's in this ad to show support in the transport of war bonds and money.

World War II. New automobiles were difficult to find, and car dealerships were forced to focus instead on maintenance and repair.

By 1942, metal scrap (mostly pots, pans, and cans) and rubber (mostly tires, shoes, raincoats, gloves, and garden hoses) drives were common. Women and school children led most of these, which served as morale boosters as much for the participants as to advance the war effort. Citizens, eager to help in any way they could, also recycled paper through paper drives. In fact, about 40 percent of all paper used during the war years was made from recycled paper.

Beer cans became beer bottles, and metal containers became glass, wood, and cardboard. Even toothpaste tubes, which were made of lead/tin alloy tubes, were collected for recycling.

Housewives saved fat scraps from meat, which they rendered, strained, cooled, and saved. They later contributed them to used fat drives to be converted into glycerin for dynamite, paint, and even Plexiglas aircraft windows. The more fat an individual turned in, the more rationing points he or she earned to buy meat.

Another way by which Americans could show their support for the war effort was by purchasing government-issued War Bonds. Usually women led the campaigns to sell them. War Bond drives—often staged as shows in which "stars" appeared—was one way of raising the public's enthusiasm. Children also participated by bringing dimes and quarters to school to buy individual stamps, which they then pasted in books. A

full book contained $18.75 worth of stamps, for example, which could be redeemed ten years later for $25.

In 1942, the federal government created the Office of Price Administration (OPA), and by 1942 it froze prices on more than half of everyday goods. The government also instigated rationing of certain goods, such as sugar and coffee, to ensure that enough supplies were available for the war effort. It distributed war ration coupon books, which shoppers took to the grocery store. At checkout, the clerk tore out the appropriate number of stamps.

Gas was another commodity rationed by the federal government. A variety of rationing stickers were provided citizens, depending on need. For example, the general public received the "A" sticker, entitling families to three gallons per week. The "B" sticker was for drivers such as traveling salesmen, who used their vehicles for their work. Ministers, postal workers, doctors, and war workers received the "C" sticker, entitling them to unlimited gasoline. Truckers received the "T" sticker for unlimited gasoline; Government officials also could pump unlimited gasoline by affixing the "X" sticker to their car windows.

In answer to gas and rubber rationing, groups organized "bicycle brigades" to conserve gas and rubber, and people walked—a lot.

Americans also helped win the war with their trowels. Since farmers were busy growing vegetables for servicemen, the government asked the public to plant vegetable gardens wherever possible—even on rooftops and in parks. An estimated 20 million

Due to rationing, toys like this Army tank were made of wood blocks and pressed particleboard.

★ ★ ★ ★ ★ ★ ★ ★ ★ ★ ★ ★ ★ ★ ★ ★ ★ ★

backyard gardens existed across the country by 1943. Not planted on a national scale since World War I, "Victory Gardens" accounted for about one-half of all vegetables consumed in the country.

The production of domestic products decreased significantly. Newspapers reduced their prints runs and page counts, but still were packed with news of the war.

Children's metal toys, such as pistols, were in significant shortage due to rationing, but makeshift versions of wood, clothes pins, paper, and cardboard worked just as well. War simulations in the streets and backyard were commonplace as children shouted not-so-polite anti-axis sentiments learned from their parents.

At the beginning of World War II, big bands, led by popular musicians such as Benny Goodman, Tommy Dorsey, Duke Ellington, dominated the American airwaves. Glenn Miller, perhaps the greatest bandleader of the era, was lost on December 15, 1944, while en route by plane over the English Channel to entertain troops in Europe. Singers such as Frank Sinatra, Bing Crosby, Frances Langford, and Perry Como, also made their mark as soloists with the big bands. The Jitterbug, known for its strenuous somersaults, splits, and twirls, allowed dancers freedom of physical expression and instituted bold styles of dress and behavior.

Music lifted spirits and energized the home front's social scene. And lyrics, as always, reflected the times. Among the many classics inspired by the war were "Boogie Woogie Bugle Boy," "Don't Sit Under the Apple Tree (with anyone else but me)," "Praise the Lord and Pass the Ammunition," "A Nightingale Sang in Berkeley Square," "The White Cliffs of Dover," and "Long Ago and Far Away."

Glenn Miller was one of the most popular big band leaders during the war. Sadly, his airplane went down over the English Channel in 1944, and he did not live to see the Allied victory.

★ ★ ★ ★ ★ ★ ★ ★ ★ ★ ★ ★ ★ ★ ★ ★ ★ ★

"MUSIC" FOR MORALE

Radio was an important source of immediate news for adults, while children enjoyed hearing 15-minute, late-afternoon programs starring fictitious heroes who chased down the enemy and saved the world. Such shows illustrated good and evil and showed how justice could prevail. The sound effects used on radio shows were addictive, and children gathered religiously around the set to listen to programs like *Captain Marvel, Little Orphan Annie,* and *Jack Armstrong.* Comic books were also entertaining and served as an affordable, portable alternative to radio. They provided a wide range of story lines for young, active imaginations.

The local movie house was also an important source of news information for the public. News shorts showing the latest film from the war fronts separated the then-common double bills. In larger cities, certain theaters played only news and feature shorts—providing a prelude to the current 24/7 television news coverage.

In the early stages of the draft, married men were exempt from war duty. Unmarried couples, worried about permanent separation, hurried to the altar, creating a marriage boom that soon became the baby boom. Incentives for women to marry also existed, as the available male population continued to diminish because of the draft.

The War Production Board restricted fabric usage in 1942, and American designers were forced to create garments that would remain stylish through several seasons. The popular zoot suit, which consisted of a high waisted, baggy-pant look for men, went quickly out of style. Women's clothes became clean cut and free of frills. Slacks became acceptable female attire, and pattern houses sold instructions for converting a man's suit into a woman's. Silk and nylon stockings virtually disappeared by 1943; instead, the fabric was used for making gunpowder bags and parachutes. Women turned to liquid leg make-up as a replacement for stockings and drew a line up the back of their legs with an eyeliner brush to give the illusion of a seam.

The Office of War Information oversaw a formal collaboration between the military and movie studios. Films, such as *Casablanca* and *Best Years of Our Lives*, were not only approved by the government but declared an important propaganda tool to boost morale. Shorts such as *It's Everybody's War*, about the effects of war on a small town, and *Who Died*, relating to War Bond support, were created to encourage Americans to take a more active role in the war.

Other memorable films produced during this era include *Mrs. Miniver, Wake Island, They Were Expendable, Story of G.I. Joe, Battle of Midway, Battle of San Pietro, Sullivan's Travels, The Miracle of Morgan's Creek,* and *Hail the Conquering Hero.*

Cartoons also contributed to the war effort through classics such as *Donald Gets Drafted* and *The New Spirit*, both released in 1942; in the latter, Donald Duck explains the importance of paying income taxes.

The inexpensive paperback book made its debut during World War II, and annual book club sales catapulted from one million to more than 10 million copies. During this period, many

Many older Americans remember comic books as an inexpensive form of entertainment during the war. But today, those same comic books aren't so cheap.

Ladies' Home Journal, July 1942, is a particularly patriotic issue, featuring pieces titled "How War Came" and "Producing For Victory," a story about how one family is living and spending their money during wartime.

writers observed the prejudices and injustices the war precipitated, and later they turned their observations into great literary works.

The December 7, 1941, attack on Pearl Harbor inspired manufacturers to package just about everything in formats they hoped would inspire patriotism. Display advertisements and magazine covers in magazines such as *Life, Collier's,* and *Ladies' Home Journal* pictured soldiers, nurses, and American flags to draw readership. Product packagers created children's games, puzzles, paper dolls, and a variety of toys and games depicting patriotic scenes, while paper items like postcards, stationery, candy boxes, and even bars of soap contained victory-related themes in red, white, and blue.

Letters sent to servicemen overseas reminded them of whom they were fighting for. When the mail arrived, an eager but anxious group gathered hoping that at least one envelope would be addressed to them.

Eastman-Kodak created V-Mail prior to the war as a lightweight form of airmail. In this process, letters were photographed, flown to their destinations, enlarged, printed, and distributed to the appropriate addresses. Other forms of V-Mail and stationery

were also used, including envelopes (referred today as "covers" by collectors) printed with propaganda slogans and embellished with patriotic or humorous graphics.

Also available to servicemen were pamphlets and leaflets printed by stationary companies, containing hints on how to write love letters and providing ideas for general correspondence for the serviceman unable to find just the right words to express his passions.

Those on the home front had access to a series of tall, narrow, folded-like-a-map, form letters, each with a humorous twist, to be sent by the creatively impaired writer to that special man overseas. They contained comic line drawings depicting servicemen in precarious situations, and their subject matter ranged from get-well wishes and birthday greetings to the general hello variety. The sender had only to address, sign, stamp, and mail it.

Pin-up girls were also popular among the men. Calendars illustrated with voluptuous young women painted by artists such as Alberto Vargas ("Varga Girls") and Gil Elvgren were the most widely distributed format. Photographic pin-ups were also popular, with Betty Grable and Rita Hayworth among the favorites.

Winston Churchill is widely credited for popularizing the "V" for Victory. When servicemen went off to war it was common for citizens to salute the troops with the "V"—a symbol made by raising the index and middle fingers.

Private and government industries used the "V" for Victory on thousands of products and promotional materials from cookbooks,

pin-back buttons, jewelry, and decals to recruiting posters and war bond ads.

The Japanese hoped to counter America's surge of patriotism with its morale-busting radio broadcasts throughout the Asian war zone by "Tokyo Rose." Thought by listeners to have been the voice of one person, "she" was actually a group of about twenty Japanese women who broadcast propaganda designed to dampen the spirits of the fighting men.

American-born "Axis Sally" was the German version. Hired by Radio Berlin, she was a single voice named Mildred Gillars. Her broadcasts often featured interviews with America G.I.'s in which she posed as a Red Cross nurse. Later, she inserted sounds of battle and propaganda messages, seriously misrepresenting the remarks of the interviewee. After the war, she was brought to trial in the United States but convicted only of broadcasting a demoralizing play. She served a prison sentence and was released in 1961.

Propaganda also was expressed in poster form. Designed to motivate and inform, among the many tag lines were admonishments to buy War Bonds, support the Red Cross, and tolerate rationing. Other posters carried Anti-Axis themes, dehumanizing the enemy through derogatory text and graphic images. Many were designed using real photographs, some with illustrations by top artists.

A 1945 patriotic booklet, *I Am An American*, contains several simple yet poetic statements that define what it is to be an American:

"I am an American. I live here. My home is here. I have friends here. My work is here. My opportunities are here. I have rights,

★ ★

privileges, duties and responsibilities here. I am proud to be an American."

Another message titled *I Believe in Democracy* reads:

"I oppose dictators because they rule by force, prevent discussion, violate conscience and suppress the people. I oppose dictators because they threaten Liberty and Freedom. My duty is to oppose dictatorship wherever it appears—in politics, government, business, industry, education, religion."

Americans will continue to enjoy freedom far into the future—but we will not maintain freedom unless we practice patriotism. For patriotism is the effort, and freedom is the result. May God bless America.

RICHARD J. PERRY

Originally used as a poster, this spectacular image is doing double time here on an Army recruitment brochure.

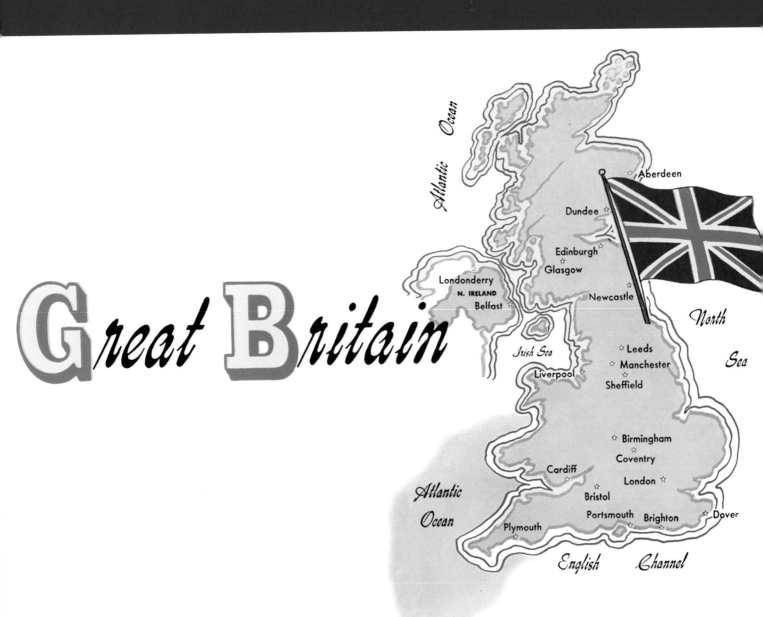

Great Britain

★ ★

Great Britain

America's entry into World War II—with its accompanying industrial power—was a welcome relief to Great Britain. Not only did Americans bring war supplies; they also brought chocolate and chewing gum—luxuries the British enjoyed immensely. Furthermore, American servicemen were a good fit with British nightlife; they usually carried pockets full of pound notes and coins to pay for their whiskey, as they didn't like British beer. Their seemingly endless access to nylon stockings made them hugely popular with the ladies.

The war imposed great hardships on the British and provided a solemn test for the fabled English stiff upper lip. The Germans continuously conducted air raids, demolishing factories, buildings, and homes. To make targeting difficult, each night the British blacked out all lights one half hour before sunset. Police and special air raid wardens strictly enforced these blackouts, knocking on the doors of violators who accidentally allowed a sliver of light to peek through a blacked-out window. Streetlights were extinguished, and even striking a match was forbidden in the early years of the war. Blackouts became as much a part of British nightlife as a thick pint of Guinness.

Due to car accidents and pedestrian mishaps the rule later was changed slightly, allowing for dimly lit torches when an air raid was not anticipated. In some towns, special night lighting was designed

★ ★

BRITISH WAR RELIEF ASSN.
OF NORTHERN CALIFORNIA
100 BUSH STREET, SAN FRANCISCO, CALIF.

THERE AIN'T NO IF'S

PLANES AND MORE PLANES

ALL TOGETHER BRITISH EMPIRE

Dentist Churchill:—"Don't worry, Old Pal, we'll 'ave a new set of teeth soon."

to shoot straight down from streetlights, thus providing pedestrians and drivers with a point of reference. But these redesigns were expensive, and not all towns were able to afford them.

Listening to the radio—for news of the war as well as entertainment—was an integral part of British life. Founded in 1922, the British Broadcasting Corporation (BBC) provided information, music, humor, and drama that the enemy couldn't block. It also offered tips on rationing and medical advice.

As did their counterparts in the U.S., movie houses played newsreels, providing updates on the war effort and how-tos on conserving goods.

Food rationing in Britain began in 1940. And with the exception of potatoes and bread, many foods eventually made the list. Although scarce, fish and sausage were not rationed, but most fruit was nearly impossible to buy. Lemons and bananas, for example, could be imported, but torpedoes fired by German U-boats often sank vessels carrying fresh food. To ensure that each person would receive an equal share of food, the government issued ration books. In order for the government to pay back its war debt and stabilize the economy, rationing in Britain didn't end until 1954.

★ ★

EXT

THE BISMARCK

North Dakota's Oldest News

ESTABLISHED 1873

BISMARCK, N. D., SUNDAY, DECEMBE

News Dispatches

from Europe and the Fa: East are subject to censorship at the source.

U.S. AT

★ ★ ★   ★ ★ ★   ★ ★ ★   ★ ★ ★ ★ ★

Pearl Harbor, Honolulu
350 Men Killed at Air B

OBSERVER SAYS 350 KILLED IN SUDDEN AIR RAID

America Goes to War in Pacific

UNION OF SOVIET SOCIALIST REPUBLICS   ALASKA

KODIAK I.   SITKA

PETROPAVLOVSK   UNALASKA   CANADA

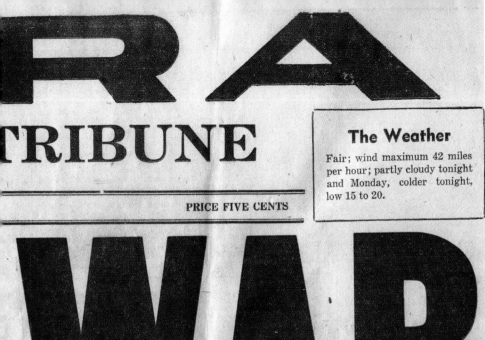

TRIBUNE

PRICE FIVE CENTS

The Weather

Fair; wind maximum 42 miles per hour; partly cloudy tonight and Monday, colder tonight, low 15 to 20.

WAR

★ ★ ★   ★ ★ ★   ★ ★ ★

ombed by Japan;
se; Warship Fired

American Victory Seen
In Big Surprise Battle

TOKYO—(AP)—Domei announced that "naval operations

The length of the war between the United States and Japan was 1,364 days, 5 hours, and 44 minutes.

LEFT: *Boys' Life*, the official magazine of the Boy Scouts of America, taught patriotism to youngsters by recruiting new troops for "duty."

RIGHT: *True Story* offered reading entertainment in the form of novelettes about real people and events to help readers pass the time. This 1942 issue focuses on life at home.

Collier's — MARCH 6, 1943 — TEN CENTS

Meet Hitler's Mind Reader in an Absorbing Novel of Nazi Germany

DOUBLE, DOUBLE, TOIL AND TROUBLE **By Lion Feu...**

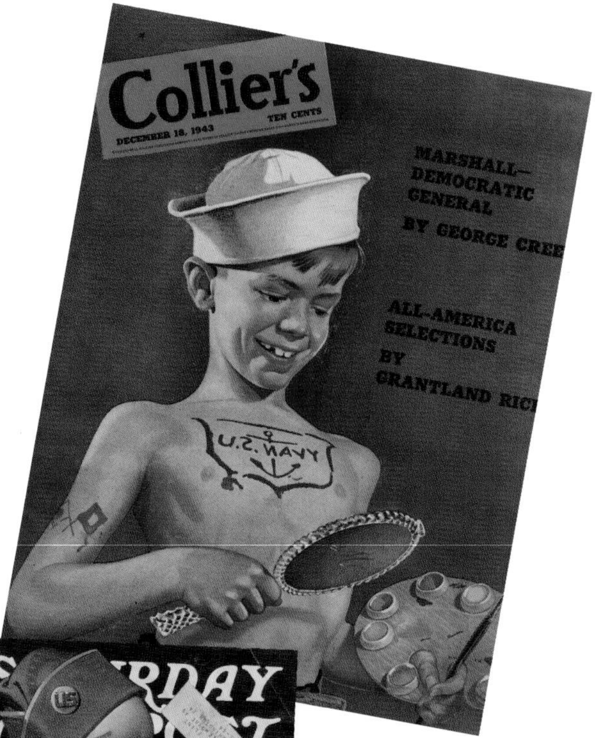

Collier's — DECEMBER 18, 1943 — TEN CENTS

MARSHALL— DEMOCRATIC GENERAL BY GEORGE CREE...

ALL-AMERICA SELECTIONS BY GRANTLAND RIC...

THE SATURDAY EVENING POST

NO TRESPASSING

1942

ABOVE LEFT: This 1943 *Collier's* cover painted by Jon Whitcomb shows that women can serve more than a hot meal and darn socks. By war's end, women were hailed for their wartime service and sacrifice.

ABOVE RIGHT: While most sailors were thinking about coming home, this youth, painted by J. C. Damron, can't wait to join!

LEFT: J. C. Leyendecker painted 322 covers for the *Saturday Evening Post*, one more than Norman Rockwell, who idolized the artist. Leyendecker's wartime babies with cheeks like apples and pudgy little limbs are among the most loved.

In November 1941, this industrial worker wears everyday work clothes. If the same man were pictured a month later, in December, he might have been wearing a military uniform.

THE SATURDAY EVENING POST

...ded A... Franklin

5c.
7c. IN CANADA

Nov. 8, '41
VOLUME 214. NUMBER 19

U.S.A.

BEGINNING MONEY IN THE BANK By P. G. WODEHOUSE

Branding was one way of showing the public a company's support of the war effort – such as this "V" for Victory Douglas Aircraft ad.

"United in this determination and with unshakable faith in the cause for which we fight, we will, with God's help, go forward to our greatest victory."

—General Dwight D. Eisenhower (1944)

Even Santa became a patriot in this 1943 Philco ad, asking people to express their spirit by buying War Bonds.

KILROY WAS HERE

KILROY IS HERE!

Kilroy Was Here was graffiti found on equipment, fences and buildings around Europe, indicating that an American GI had been there.

Give Him Wings!

Buy Those Bonds Now!

Here's a pair of happy sailors posing for a snapshot while on leave with their girlfriends. The author's father is on the right.

OUR GREAT

GENERAL MacARTHUR

100 LARTZ

Victory **Photo Corners**

IN OUR COUNTRY'S COLORS:
RED, WHITE & BLUE

Lieutenant Walter Lartz U.S.A.

Have You a Son or Sweetheart

Soldier   Sailor   Pilot or Mar...

Save his pictures with his colors—
Red, White and Blue—and
"Whip Our Foe—Keep US Champs—
Buy Your Country's Bonds and Stamps

© 1942 LARTZ   SURING, WIS., U.S....

This image of Gen. Douglas MacArthur was a popular print used on items ranging from calendars to thermometers.

CRESCENT CLEANERS
LOUIS KEMP, Owner
Master Cleaners for those who Demand the Best
3rd & Walnut   Spokane
Phone Riv. 2345

The **V**ICTORY
Garden Spray Nozzle

Dense, Misty Spray . . .
Gives Young, Growing
Plants the Right Start

10¢

Fan Spray Fits All Garden Hose

H. B. SHERMAN MANUFACTURING CO.

PLEDGE
OF ALLEGIANCE
I Pledge allegiance to
the flag of the United States
of America, and to the
Republic for which
it stands: one nation, indivisible, with liberty and
justice for all.

FREEDOM
AND
JUSTICE
FOR ALL

UNITED
WE
STAND

PLEDGE
OF ALLEGIANCE
I Pledge allegiance to
the flag of the United S

Compact fans,
like these two
examples, were
popular accessories
for social events.

"We played war often as kids. We'd take a stick of wood, a clothespin, and an old rubber bicycle tire and make a play gun. We chased each other up and down the streets for hours."

—Bill Johnson, Los Angeles, CA

World War II scrapbooks, such as this one, are becoming scarce. And the collector has scored a real prize when he finds one containing newspaper clippings, prints, photos, greeting cards, and letters.

Cracker Jacks contained only military-related prizes during the United States involvement during World War II.

Paper cut-out dolls were an inexpensive alternative for children whose "real" dolls were produced in fewer numbers during World War II. These examples were among the most patriotic available.

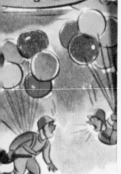

JUST LOVES DESSERT, CAPTAIN,
I SEE THAT HE EATS HIS VEGETABLES!
COPYRIGHT 1942 BY AMERICAN ART SERVICE

"GUESS WHO?"
COPYRIGHT 1942 BY AMERICAN ART SERVICE

BONG!

S.P.

HE COOKIES. THE ONE I
Z BY AMERICA

"HOPE I'M CALLED SOON—I'M CRAZY
INTO A UNIFORM!"
ART SERVICE

DMIRED THESE STRIPES ON
W—SO I GOT SOME FOR
COPYRIG

"I'M OUT TO WIN THE SCRA
OUR DIVISION!"

IT IS YOUR PATRIOTIC DUTY TO write V TO THE BOYS IN OUR ARMED FORCES

OLD GLORY

ONE NATION INDIVISIBLE 1943-44

COUNCIL AGAINST INTOLERANCE IN AMERICA

A VISUAL JOURNEY OF WARTIME PATRIOTISM ★ 45

V-mail letters were a perfectly reduced photograph of an original letter, weighing 140 times less!

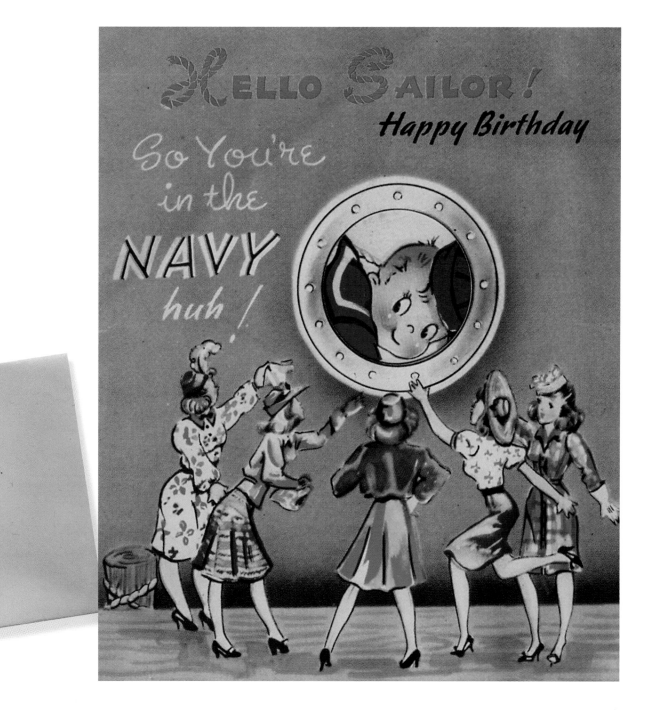

• CONTENTS •
PHOTOGRAPHIC SAFETY FILM
NOT DANGEROUS

WAR & NAVY
DEPARTMENTS
V····MAIL SERVICE
OFFICIAL BUSINESS

PENALTY FOR
PRIVATE USE TO
AVOID PAYMENT OF
POSTAGE, $300

V····-MAIL
STATION

V····MAIL

RUSH

Exact Size of V-Mail Box When Folded to Its Original Size of
4"x4", Contains 1750 Letters in 16mm Film Weighing 4 Ozs.

Don't need schooling to know how to handle these figures—Seven lovely WAVES plus seven mail bags full of letters for the fighting Bluejackets overseas equal two vivacious sweethearts holding one V-Mail bag (of V-Mail letters) which contains all the letters originally in the seven bags. Shown holding the mail bags are (left to right): Sp(M)3c Helen Robertson, Sp(M)3c Maria Berg, Sp(M)3c Genevieve DeLaney, Y3c Bernice Wanagee, Sp(M)3c Carlwyn Cameron, Y2c LaVonne Cobble and Y3c Edith Worthen.

Yep, the V-Mail is a part of the precious cargo destined to bring "learn light" and glaring smiles to those fighting Bluejackets who are deliverin that will eventually spell doom for all foes of democracy. Judging from smiles of these two winsome WAVES, Lt. (jg) Cecelia Simon and Sp(M)3c find it a distinct pleasure to serve in their capacity at the Fleet Post V-Mail division.

1750 V-MAIL LETTERS WEIGH F
OUNCES — GO BY FAST PLAN

PHOTOGRAPHED IN YOUR OWN HANDWRI
V-MAIL BRINGS A PERSONALIZED MESSAG

Open skies . . . and the drone of an approachi
stirs the silence. Below on "Operations—", men wat
ly as they wait to identify the nearing craft. This
it! Watchers relax as the steady hum becomes a r
head. Broad smiles are suddenly the order of the
figures dash from all directions, spreading the n
cargo plane! . . . Supplies desperately needed, neces
a little more than mere existence . . . and mail! Fo
the ever growing link between the man in that iso
point on the map and his folks back in Everytown,

A constant stream of supplies is being sent to t
lying stations and space is so vitally important now
portant because every beachhead must be held by equipment
from home. Thus the line leads directly to that small brown
V-Mail envelope . . . V-Mail providing precious connections
from one side of the world to the other . . . exchange of
"news and views" from you to me . . . and vice versa!

Each V-Mail letter is a perfectly reduced photograph
of the original. Johnny out there is pretty pleased when he
sees that familiar writing. He probably doesn't stop to con-
sider the process that makes his letter available . . . much
too busy. However, when the first miniature V-Mail letter
from Johnny was placed in the box at home, it created a lot
of notice and his dad, being of an inquiring mind, started a
bit of an investigation.

Result—John, Sr., discovered the whole idea to be . . .
"solid" . . . practical and here to stay.

John, Sr., was right. A letter written on a V-Mail form
in anyone of the following:
DARK INK— HEAVY PENCIL— TYPEWRITTEN—
is easily photographed . . . Imagine 1750 letters only weighing four ounces of film—carry an A-1 priority and go by
fast plane to the war areas. The V-Mail negatives are then
printed and swiftly delivered . . . and another bluejacket
knows he is not so far away after all.

V "WHAT MAKES

DID YOU KNOW!!

V-MAIL letters weigh
140 times less than a stand-
ard letter, and save 98 per
cent in cargo space.

V-Mail Is Vital Mail
Carries A-1 Priority
Overseas by Fast
Plane.

(Reprinted from "The Masthead") YANK(?)—9-15-44—6OE—311.

ON TO VICTORY
FOR LIBERTY!

© J. M., N.Y., 1942

STAMP EM OUT!

© J. M., N.Y., 1942

'm Working with
Uncle Sam!

© J. M., N.Y., 1942

DO YOUR SHARE FOR FREEDOM

AND VICTORY WILL BE OURS!

© J. M., N.Y., 1942

15
SHEETS

PATRIOTIC WRITING PAPER

ALL DIFFERENT PRIZE WINNING DESIGNS AND
SLOGANS THAT WON IN A NATIONAL CONTEST

10
CENTS

KEEP THAT LIGHT BURNING!

© J. M., N.Y., 1942

TODAY··MORE THAN EVER

AND THAT GOVERNMENT OF THE PEOPLE,
BY THE PEOPLE, FOR THE PEOPLE, SHALL
NOT PERISH FROM THE EARTH.

FROM LINCOLN'S GETTYSBURG ADDRESS

© J. M., N.Y., 1942

LET
FREEDOM
RING
for
ALL THE WORLD

© J. M., N.Y., 1942

"LIFE, LIBERTY
AND THE PURSUIT
OF HAPPINESS"

Th Jefferson

© J. M., N.Y., 1942

LIBERTY
ABOVE ALL·FOR ALL

© J. M., N.Y., 1942

United for VICTORY

© J. M., N.Y., 1942

GOD BLESS OUR BOYS

God bless our boys,
    God keep them safe
Wherever they may be
    As valiantly
    they carry on
The fight for liberty.

God keep them ever strong
    in faith,
God keep their courage high
And grant them, too,
    a fearlessness,
A will that cannot die.

They do not fight alone --
    Our Boys --
They're in our every prayer,
God guide them and
    protect them all
And keep them in His care.

COPYRIGHT 1942
HALL BROTHERS, INC.

A HALLMARK MOTTO

Toward Peace and Happiness

Season's G

TO A SERVICE MOTHER

A Mother's Day Message

"Tires were real difficult to get so my dad would jack up the car to add miles so we would get new tires. You got a pair of tires for so many miles you traveled."

—Frank Maxwell, Junction City, OR

VICTORY
starts in the
AMERICAN KITCHEN

RED CROSS NUTRITIONISTS
teach
HOW FOODS BUILD
BUOYANT HEALTH

Enroll NOW
RED CROSS NUTRITION COURSE

Packed with hundreds of recipes and tips for conserving rationing point coupons, food, money, and time, this victory cookbook is a virtual advertising memorial for most major food brands of the day.

U.S. FOOD
ADMINISTRATION

EAT MORE
CORN, OATS AND **RYE PRODUCTS —** **FISH** AND **POULTRY —** **FRUITS, VEGETABLES** AND **POTATOES BAKED, BOILED** AND **BROILED FOODS**

EAT LESS
WHEAT, MEAT, SUGAR AND **FATS**

TO SAVE FOR THE ARMY AND OUR ALLIES

POTATOES HAVE ENLISTED TO LICK THE AXIS

INCREASE PRODUCTION PER ACRE
REDUCE ROUGH HANDLING
MORE U. S. NO. 1 POTATOES

AGRICULTURAL DEVELOPMENT DEPARTMENT
UNION PACIFIC RAILROAD

ELIMINATE WASTE

MEAT IS AMMUNITION

INCREASE NUMBER ON FEED
FEED FOR HEAVIER WEIGHTS
REDUCE LOSS IN SHIPPING
CONTROL DISEASES

AGRICULTURAL DEVELOPMENT DEPARTMENT
UNION PACIFIC RAILROAD

ELIMINATE WASTE

"Everyone in town had a huge garden. Tomatoes were put up for winter, and lined up in the basement. I remember many meals of just corn on the cob. We consumed as little as possible."

—Jack Kostel, Tyndall, SD

FORWARD
...all along the line!

AMERICA is on the offensive wherever the flag flies . . . for one purpose, and one purpose only—to bring this war to a victorious close as quickly as possible.

If this is to be the year, as everybody hopes, then the call is not only for *united* effort—but for that extra "something" from every American on the home front. Count on the 161,922 workers of the Pennsylvania Railroad to do their share!

Count on them to help keep rolling the greatest volume of freight and passenger traffic in the history of railroading...to push war shipments through with speed and efficiency...and to serve the traveling public in the spirit of courtesy and friendliness characteristic of the Pennsylvania Railroad at *all* times—in war or peace.

Pennsylvania Railroad
Serving the Nation

★ 37,960 in the Armed Forces   ★ 81 have given their lives for their country

BUY UNITED STATES WAR BONDS AND STAMPS

The Pennsylvania Railroad got into the act with this graphically moving ad urging the purchase of War Bonds and Stamps.

SAY YES!

Take your change in **WAR STAMPS**

On commission from the U.S. government, many artists designed posters, which were meant to promote numerous causes. Among them were admonishments to buy War Bonds, grow Victory Gardens, and join forces to end the war—the latter was particularly effective in encouraging trained nurses and young men and women to join the ranks. Such posters were considered ephemera and thus discarded after the war. Remaining examples continue to grow in value.

The staff of Foster and Kleiser, the famed Los Angeles billboard company, poses in front of their newest billboard creation, which they donated to the war effort.

"One front and one battle where everyone in the United States—every man, woman, and child is in action. That front is right here at home, in our daily lives."

—Franklin Delano Roosevelt, 32nd President of the United States, April 1942, addressing the nation

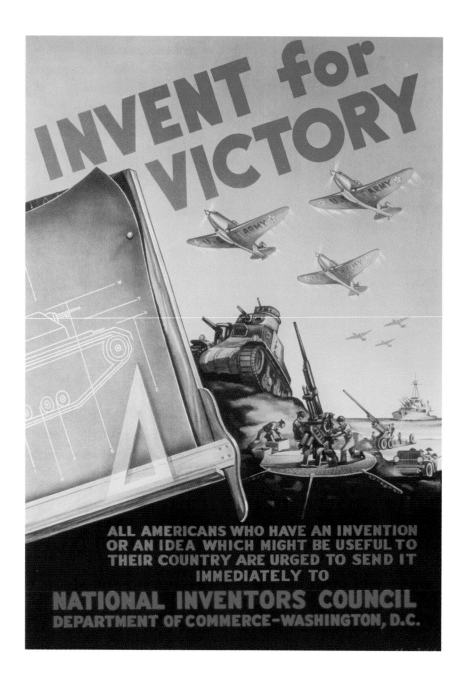

INVENT for VICTORY

ALL AMERICANS WHO HAVE AN INVENTION OR AN IDEA WHICH MIGHT BE USEFUL TO THEIR COUNTRY ARE URGED TO SEND IT IMMEDIATELY TO

NATIONAL INVENTORS COUNCIL
DEPARTMENT OF COMMERCE—WASHINGTON, D.C.

Isn't it great to be an American

WAR WORKER **V**

The weight of the chain—more than four times the length necessary to reach the ocean's bottom—and not the weight of the anchor itself keeps a ship anchored.

BUY WAR BONDS

"I remember the day we (the Armed Forces) entered Europe. There was high anxiety in our family ... we had half a dozen (family members) there. We'd nearly fight to get to the radio to hear about the war."—Cecil Sims, Mineola, TX

Are you a girl with a Star-Spangled heart?

JOIN THE WAC NOW

THOUSANDS OF ARMY JOBS NEED FILLING!

Women's Army Corps
United States Army

SILENCE MEANS SECURITY

WAAC

THIS IS MY WAR TOO!
WOMEN'S ARMY AUXILIARY CORPS
UNITED · STATES · ARMY

"Victory Girl" was the title bestowed upon single women who were coping with the stateside shortage of men. It also was applied to some unscrupulous married women whose husbands were overseas fighting the war.

REMEMB[ER]

V

PEAR[L]

HARBO[R]

"I know not with
what weapons
World War III will
be fought, but
World War IV
will be fought
with sticks
and stones."

—Albert Einstein,
U.S. physicist, born in
Germany; formulated
theory of relativity

1778

1943

BOOKS WANTED
FOR OUR MEN
IN CAMP AND
"OVER THERE"
TAKE YOUR GIFTS TO
THE PUBLIC LIBRARY

AMERICANS
will _always_ fight for liberty

IT'S UP TO YOU

PROTECT THE
NATION'S HONOR
— ENLIST NOW —
ASSOCIATED MOTION PICTURE ADVERTISERS

Mussolini coined the name "Axis," meaning to communicate that these countries comprised the central point around which other European countries would exist. The Axis countries were Germany, Austria, Italy, Hungary, Bulgaria, Rumania, Finland, and, later in the war, Japan.

I WANT YOU

for the U.S. ARMY
ENLIST NOW

Service as a submariner is glorified in this recruitment brochure. "For your comfort, each leather-covered bunk has excellent springs and a soft, restful mattress . . . an automatic washing machine and record player . . . and the food . . . is the envy of the fleet!"

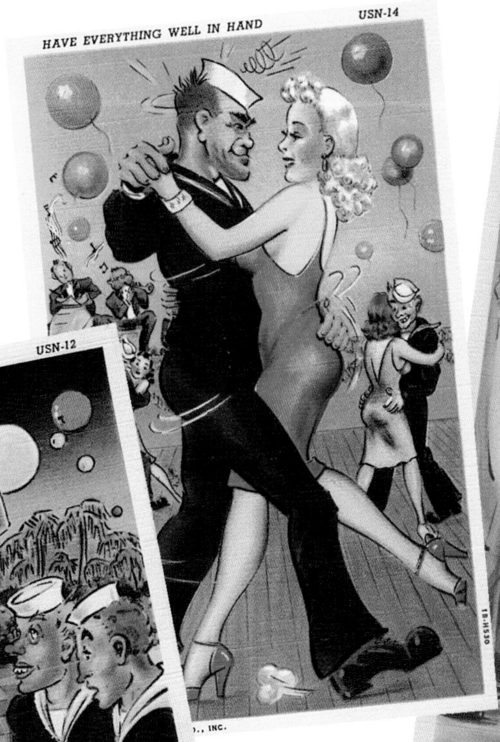

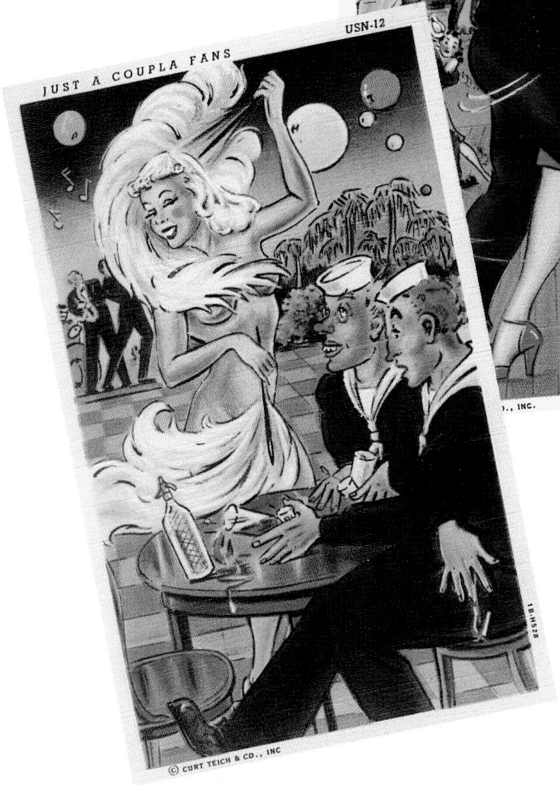

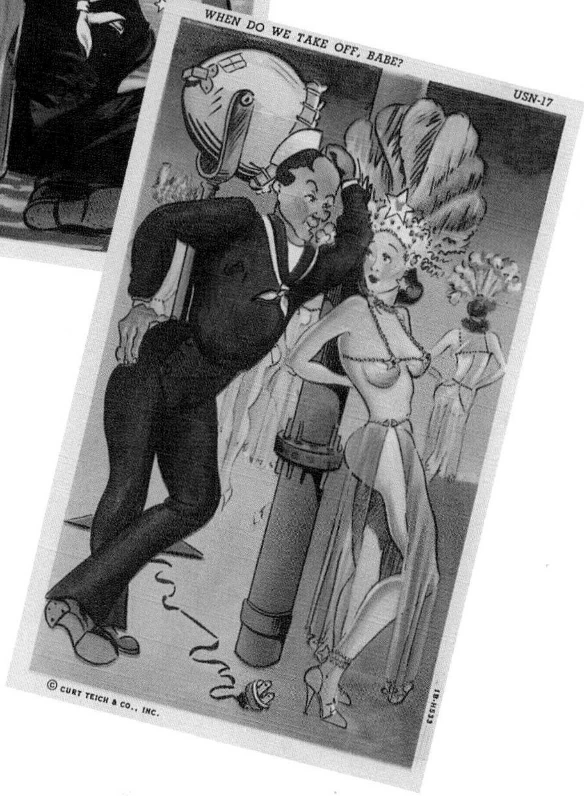

HAVE EVERYTHING WELL IN HAND
USN-14

FRESH!
USN-13
LULU
THE GREAT
MIND READER
© CURT TEICH & CO., INC.

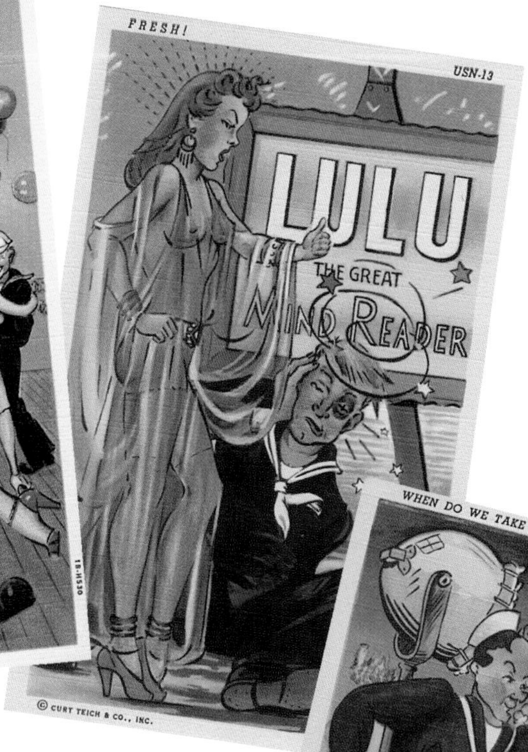

JUST A COUPLA FANS
USN-12
© CURT TEICH & CO., INC

WHEN DO WE TAKE OFF, BABE?
USN-17
© CURT TEICH & CO., INC.

It was common for servicemen to send comic postcards to their families. In a message on the back of the card, the writer often compared the card's recipient to the character(s) pictured on the card.

"You ask, what is our aim? I can answer in one word. It is victory. Victory at all costs. Victory in spite of all terrors. Victory, however long and hard the road may be, for without victory there is no survival."

—Winston Churchill,
British statesman and writer; Prime Minister

THE NAVY CERTAINLY IS IN PRETTY GOOD SHAPE!

THINK OF ME, ALL AT SEA, FEELING SO BLUE — AND WONDERING IF YOU ARE TRUE!

YOU'RE IN THE ARMY NOW—AND HOW!

LEFT FACE!
PORT ARMS!
COMP'NY HALT!
PRESENT ARMS!

RIGHT FACE!
LEFT OBLIQUE MARCH!
ORDER ARMS!
COUNT OFF!

A "K Ration" was a packet of food issued to soldiers, containing items such as corned pork loaf, milk tablets, bouillon, sugar, and instant coffee. Boxes were marked "breakfast," "lunch," or "dinner," and kept their contents varied accordingly.

NO FAIR RACIN'— I'VE GOT TO SHAVE GOITY, TOO!

"No bastard has ever won a war by dying for his country. He won it by making the other poor dumb bastard die for his country."

—George S. Patton, Jr., U.S. General

V7

(C) 1941 Tichnor Bros., Inc.

"We are determined that before the sun sets on this terrible struggle our flag will be recognized throughout the world as a symbol of freedom on the one hand, of overwhelming power on the other."

—George C. Marshall, U.S. General and statesman; U.S. Army Chief of Staff; Secretary of State; originator of the Marshall Plan for economic recovery in Europe, following world War II

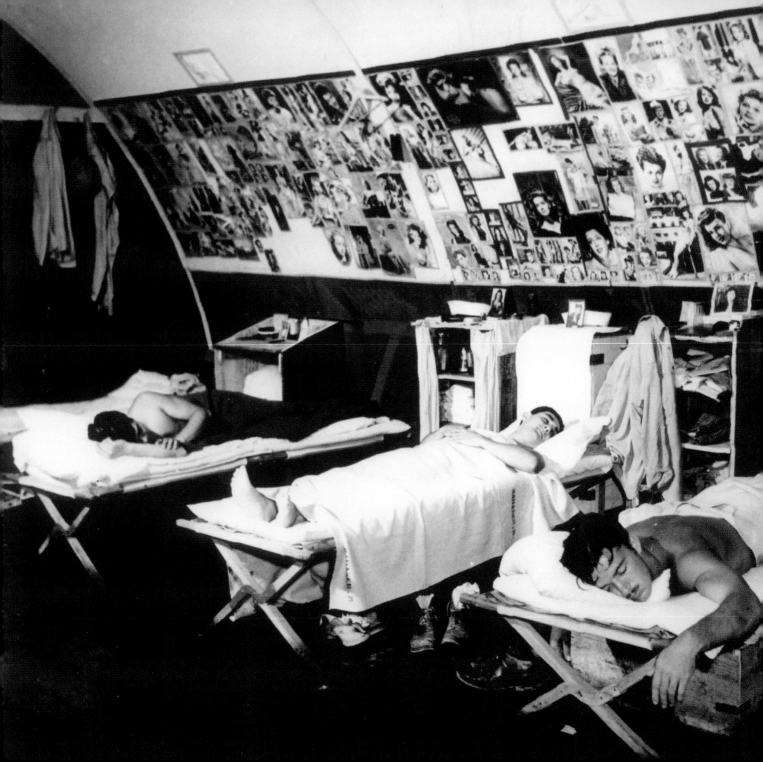

The High Sign

Photographs of actresses, singers, and models were common décor among the troops, serving as reminders of home and the cause. Pin-up illustrations by artists such as Alberto Vargas (Varga Girls), Gil Elvgren, and Earl Moran were colorful alternatives to real photos and are highly collectible today.

"G.I." was derived from the words
"Government Issue," a term used to identify
American servicemen's equipment.

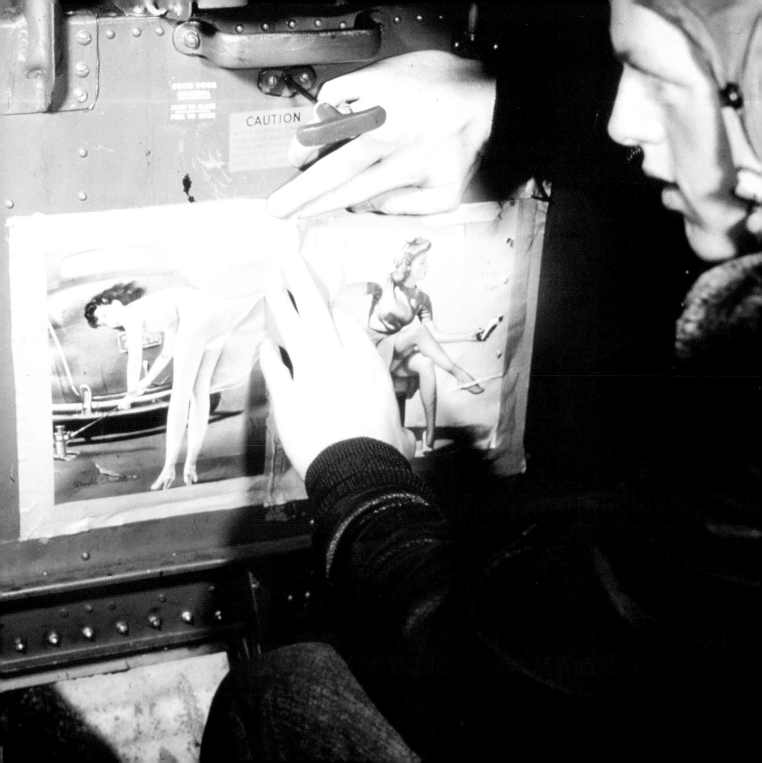

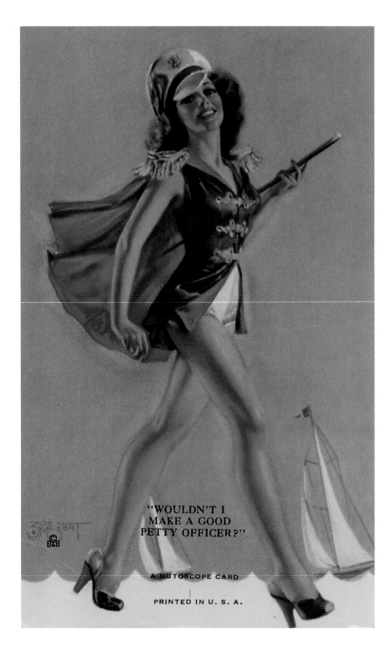

"WOULDN'T I
MAKE A GOOD
PETTY OFFICER?"

A MUTOSCOPE CARD

PRINTED IN U. S. A.

Going My Way

del Masters

© LITHO U.S.A.

ANKLES AWEIGH

A B-17 named All American established the aircraft's reputation for durability when it was nearly sliced in half in a collision with a German plane. It managed to stay airborne and return to base. But upon landing, a serviceman opened an exit hatch and the plane instantly broke in half.

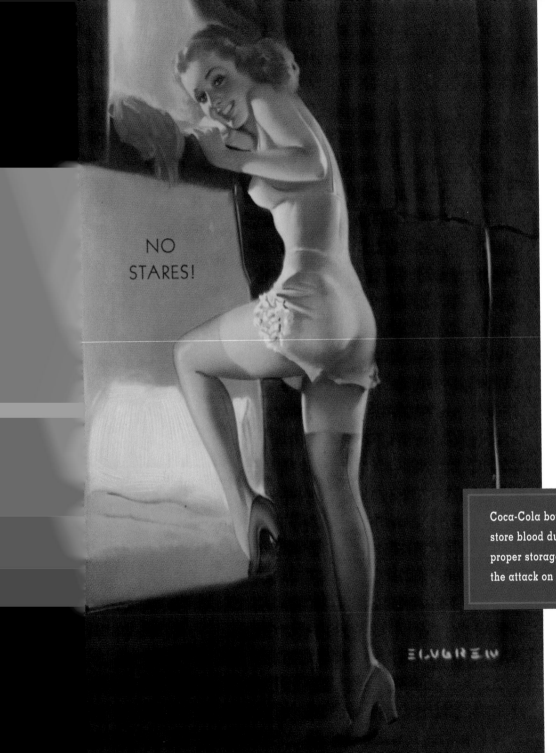

NO
STARES!

ELVGREN

Coca-Cola bottles were used to
store blood due to a shortage of
proper storage containers during
the attack on Pearl Harbor.

GOD BLESS
AMERICA

1942

American NOT American't

VISIBILITY PERFECT

A MUTOSCOPE CARD

A MUTOSCOPE CARD

PRINTED IN U. S. A.

> "Ace" was a term given to a
> pilot who shot down five enemy
> aircraft. Less than one percent of
> all pilots became one, yet nearly
> half of all downed aircraft were at
> the hands of an Ace.

SPORT MODEL

AND STILL THE MOST POPULAR BOOK MATCHES IN AMERICA

NO UNION LABEL

Please do NOT ask us to print the Union Label on Elvgren Matches; cannot be had at any price.

PRICE LIST
Order By No. G-914

Quantity	Price	Deposit	Balance
2,500	$ 9.95	$ 2.00	$ 7.95
5,000	18.45	3.00	15.45
7,500	27.45	4.00	23.45
10,000	35.40	5.00	30.40
15,000	52.30	7.00	45.30
25,000	84.95	10.00	74.95
50,000	157.50	14.00	143.50
100,000	300.00	20.00	280.00

Pay Only Deposits as Shown; Balance C.O.D., Plus Delivery Charges
PRICES INCLUDE FEDERAL EXCISE TAX OF $1.00 PER CASE
of 2,500 Matches
SOLD F. O. B. CHICAGO ONLY

NO 1,000 ORDERS

Elvgren Book Matches sold in minimum lots of one case (2,500). No 1,000 orders can be accepted.

CLOSE COVER FOR SAFETY
SOUTH SAN FRANCISCO LIQUOR STORE
John & Joe Penna, Props.
Imported and Domestic WINES AND LIQUORS
379 GRAND AVE.
South San Francisco, Calif.
Phone S. F. 1856
UP TO PAR
National Press, Chicago

UP TO PAR

ASSORTED ONLY ON SMALL ORDERS

All orders for less than 25,000 Elvgren Matches will be filled with an EQUAL quantity of ALL FIVE SUBJECTS. Customers may specify one, two or more pictures ONLY when ordering 25,000 or more, and as long as selection is made in even units of 2,500. THESE MATCHES MAY ALSO BE PURCHASED ON A CONTRACT BASIS, but only at the prices shown above.

CLOSE COVER FOR SAFETY
THE CAMEL CLUB
SAILOR'S HAVEN
1034 KEARNY ST.
JUST UP THE HUMP FROM INT. SETTLEMENT
San Francisco, Calif.
Phone EX. 9591
GOOD PICKIN'S
National Press, Chicago

GOOD PICKIN'S

LET'S GO U.S.A.
KEEP 'EM ROLLING

SUGGESTION FOR INSIDE COVER

CLOSE COVER FOR SAFETY
Moderne BEAUTY SALON
For Appointment Call FU. 7442
828-29-30 MIAMI SAVINGS BLDG.
MISS LOU WILLIAMS
FU. 7442
DAYTON, OHIO
CAUGHT IN THE DRAFT
National Press, Chicago

CAUGHT IN THE DRAFT

CLOSE COVER FOR SAFETY
THE FRIENDLY TAVERN
WM. F. KNOLL, Prop.
Phone: L. S. 773
ERIAL ROAD
PINE HILL, N. J.
OPEN SUNDAYS
FOIL PROOF
National Press, Chicago

FOIL PROOF

CLOSE COVER FOR SAFETY
HARRY'S GRILL
DINE and DANCE
Every Friday and Saturday
FREE PARKING
3029 WEST 117TH ST.
CLEVELAND, OHIO
Phone CL. 9874
KEEP 'EM FLYING
National Press, Chicago

KEEP 'EM FLYING

V
REMEMBER PEARL HARBOR

SUGGESTION FOR INSIDE COVER

V
REMEMBER PEARL HARBOR

INSIDE COVERS

AMOUNT OF COPY WE CAN PRINT

Copy should be confined to three or four lines as shown; with a saddle slogan or copy in one or two lines as indicated by these samples. On the INSIDE covers we recommend one of our regular book match illustrations, a couple of saddle slogans, or customers own copy in six to eight lines. Crowded copy means poor advertising; keep message brief and to the point for the best results.

Keep 'Em Flying!

LIGHTNING INTERCEPTOR

SURE do wish that you were here
To brighten up the place
MISS you like the dickens
'Cause you surely are on ace!
IF you get a minute free
And haven't much to do —
LIKE it if you'd write to me
And tell me all that's new.
EVERYBODY'S feeling fine
And send their best regards
Oh, yes — and here's a brand new SMILE
To give to all your pards!

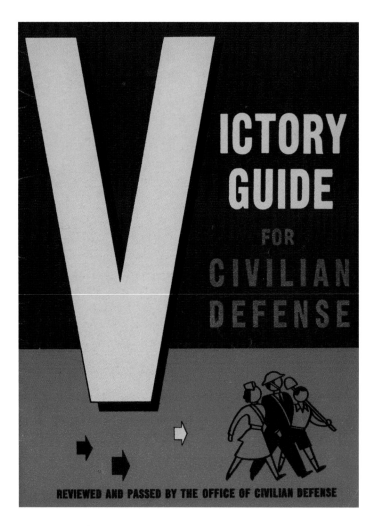

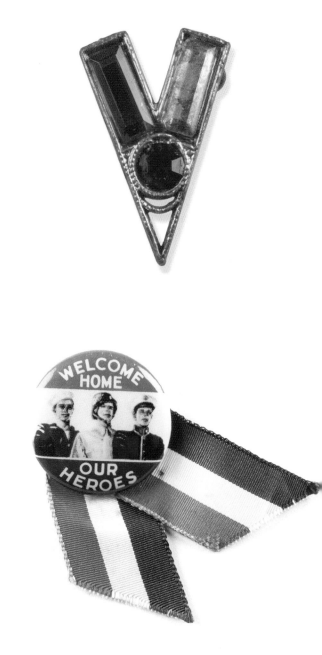

"We raised our own meat and vegetables. We didn't need butter so we traded butter stamps for sugar stamps with my aunt. I remember faithfully saving shortening and meat drippings and taking them to the meat market. " —Margaret Nicholson, Kewanee, IL

THE ETUDE

July 1942

music magazine

Price 25 Cents

UNITED WE STAND

"Sunday night was a special night for the whole family. Jack Benny was on (the radio). Everyone in the country knew the same comics and songs. Radio was important in those days." —Charles Sharp, Frankfurt, IN

Music always brings a sense of community to our lives. Patriotic songs in particular were immensely popular during the war. Songs like "Star Spangled Banner" and "America, the Beautiful," written long before the war, remain classics today, while "Any Bonds Today" by Irving Berlin, given free in sheet-music format by the Treasury Department to promote the purchase of war bonds, has faded away in popularity.

THE ETUDE

July
1940

Price 25 Cents

music magazine

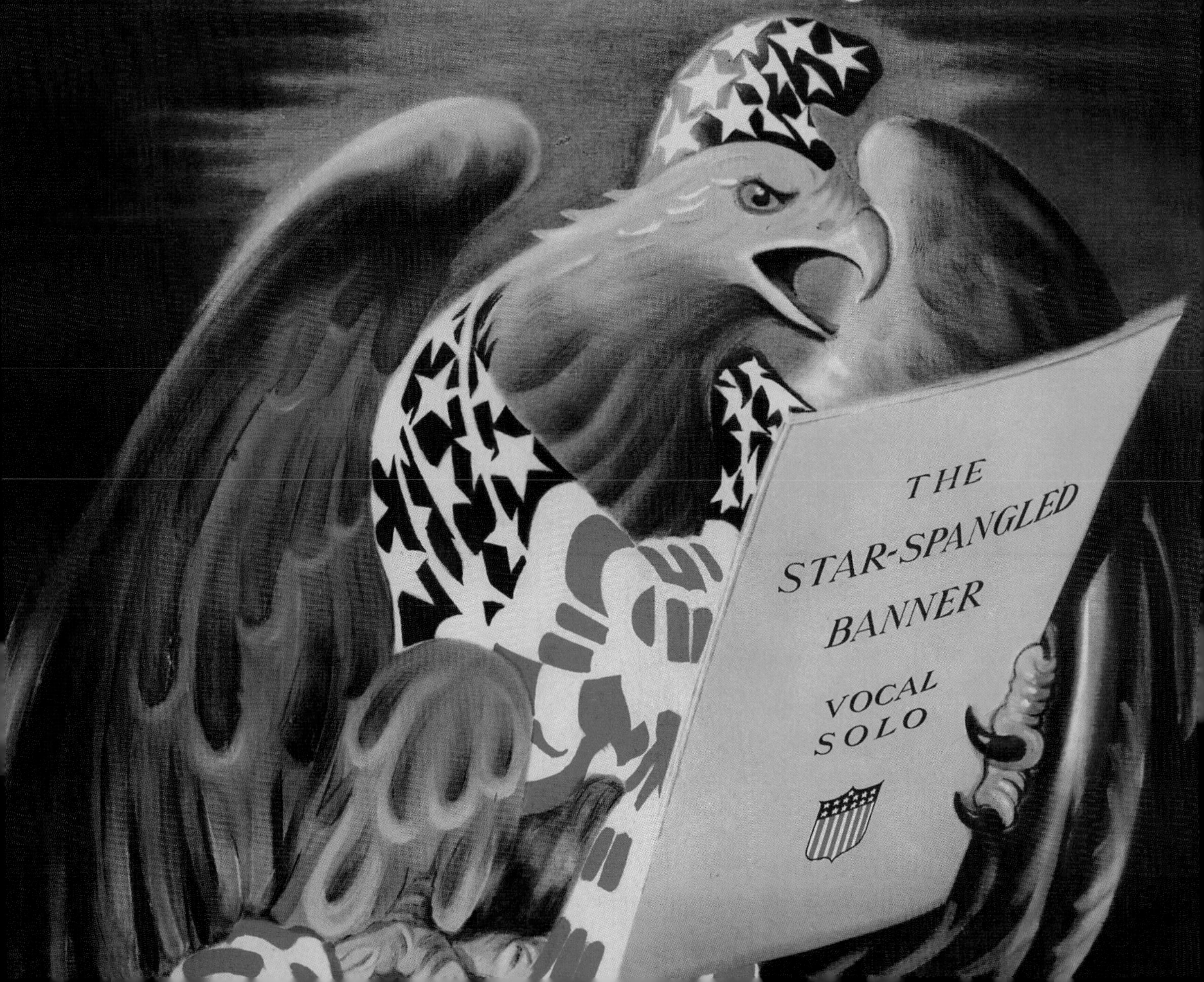

Between 1939 and 1943 the Nobel
Peace Prize was not awarded as no
candidates could be found.

"Sweethearts" of servicemen and others with a patriotic sense often added sweetheart jewelry to their ensembles. The pins came in many shapes and sizes, usually symbolizing a branch of service or other patriotic icon. Versions with red-white-and-blue rhinestones were among the most popular, but simple designs were also enjoyed.

"There were lots of radio programs in the late afternoon. I listened to Dick Tracy. I had a decoder pen that you ordered (by mail) in order to solve the mystery."

—Len Stoffer, Portland, OR

TAKEN

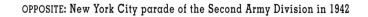
OPPOSITE: New York City parade of the Second Army Division in 1942

"Movies were real big. Everyone went once a week. We had three theaters but only about 16,000 people. We always got a newsreel and a cartoon... five to six minutes (before the feature film) . . . starting with the war . . . then it went local."

—Charles Sharp, Frankfurt, IN

During World War II, sauerkraut was referred to as "liberty cabbage," and hamburger became known as "liberty steak."

"We couldn't get butter at all. We would get the ration coupons, then go to the store and buy margarine. You used a small pack of yellow coloring and worked it into the margarine to make it look like butter. Then you could add a can of Pet milk and work that in and it would almost taste like butter." —Cathy Bowden, Dallas, TX

...we here highly resolve that these dead shall not have died in vain...

REMEMBER DEC. 7th!

"My uncle came rushing into the room (we never locked doors back then) yelling 'the Japanese bombed Pearl Harbor' and said 'I'm joining the navy!' and then he ran out of the room."

—Jack Kostel, Tyndall, SD

ON TO VICTORY - *Sinking of the Haruna*

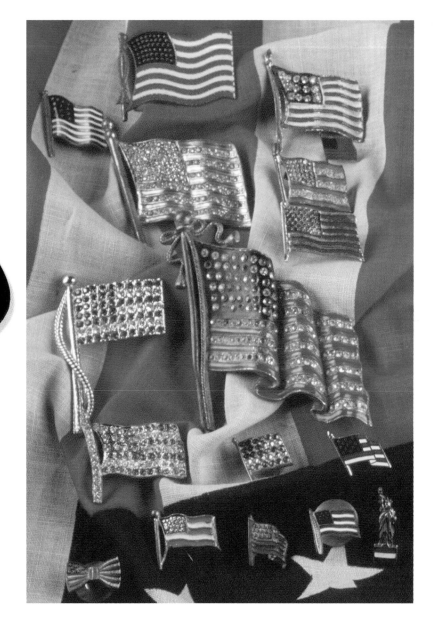

The only sports banned during World War II were horse racing (because it was non-essential) and auto racing (which used rubber and gas).

"KEEP HER FLYING"

We have pledged our share in U.S. DEFENSE BONDS and STAMPS!

★ ★ HAVE YOU? ★ ★

COURTESY LIPMAN WOLFE & CO.

The U.S. Army created a budget version of Spam for the military that was inferior in quality to the version popularized during World War II.

Tuesday was the day America was asked to not eat meat as part of the rationing effort.

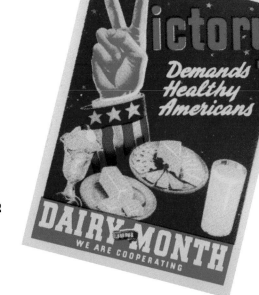

RATIONED ITEMS IN THE U.S.

Rubber January 15, 1942

Civilian cars February 2, 1942

Typewriters March 24, 1942

Bicycles and gasoline May 15, 1942

Farm machinery September 15, 1942

Rubber boots October 5, 1942

Fuel oil October 22, 1942

Milk cans and farm fences November 11, 1942

Coffee November 29, 1942

Coal and oil stoves December 18, 1942

Shoes February 7, 1943

Processed foods and firewood March 1, 1943

Canned milk June 2, 1943

Soft cheese June 6, 1943

PLEDGE

TO EVERY SOLDIER, SAILOR
AND MARINE WHO IS FIGHTING
FOR MY COUNTRY

For you there can be no rest.
For me there should be no
vacation from the part I can
play to help win the war. I
therefore solemnly promise to
continue to buy United States
War Savings Stamps and Bonds
to the limit of my ability,
throughout my summer vacation
and until our Victory is won.

Jim Kluge

Witnessed by Lulu Hurst   Dated May 29, '42

This Pledge certificate, printed by the U.S. government,
served as an agreement to buy war savings stamps and
bonds until victory was achieved.

We gave!
COMMUNITY CHEST

GIVE TO
USO
UNITED SERVICE ORGANIZATIONS

Calendars were widely distributed during the war. Examples
such as this were common in homes. Overseas you would find less
wholesome examples of the girl-next-door.

The Veterans' Service Magazine provided everything
one would need to know to correctly display the flag.
And citizens did—by the tens of thousands.

Make and Mend was a sewing-tip book, providing
the Rosie who wasn't a riveter methods and tips on
turning those knockabouts into knockouts.

THE NATIONAL ANTHEM

Oh say, can you see, by the dawn's early light,
What so proudly we hailed at the twilight's last gleaming?
Whose broad stripes and bright stars, through the perilous fight,
O'er the ramparts we watched, were so gallantly streaming!
And the rockets' red glare, the bombs bursting in air,
Gave proof through the night that our flag was still there:
Oh say, does that star-spangled banner yet wave
O'er the land of the free and the home of the brave?

RIGHT: Battle maps, such as this 1943 example, were used to inform the home front of the war's progress worldwide, and often "projected" where battles would be won.

"It is my earnest hope—indeed the hope of all mankind—that from this solemn occasion a better world shall emerge out of the blood and carnage of the past, a world founded upon faith and understanding, a world dedicated to the dignity of man and the fulfillment of his most cherished wish for freedom, tolerance, and justice."

—Douglas MacArthur
U.S. General; Commander in Chief of Allied Forces
in the Southwest Pacific, World War II (1945)

INVASION and TOTAL WAR VICTORY MAPS

with DECORATIONS, ILLUSTRATIONS and MILITARY and NAVAL INSIGNIA

The
PLEDGE TO THE
Flag

I pledge allegiance to the flag
of the United States
of America,
And to the Republic
for which it stands,
One Nation, indivisible,
With liberty and
justice for all.

Issued two years prior to the U.S.
involvement in World War II, "How to
Display and Respect Our Flag" shows
the following as the official dates to
display the flag:

January 20: Every four years, the president is inaugurated on this day.

February 12: Lincoln's birthday

February 22: Washington's birthday

April 6: Army Day (anniversary of U.S.
entrance into World War I in 1917)

Second Sunday in May: Mother's Day

Third Sunday in May: "I Am An
American Citizenship Day"

May 30: Memorial Day (flag half-masted
until noon, full-masted rest of
day), subsequently changed to the
last Monday in May.

June 14: Flag Day

July 4: Independence Day

August 19: National Aviation Day

First Monday in September: Labor Day

September 14: Anniversary of writing of "Star Spangled Banner"
in 1814

September 17: Constitution Day (anniversary of the adoption of
the Constitution in 1787)

Last Day in September: Gold Star Mother's Day (A Gold Star
Mother was one who had lost a child in war)

October 12: Columbus Day, subsequently changed to second
Monday in October

October 27: Navy Day (birthday of Theodore Roosevelt)

First Tuesday after the first Monday in November in 1944, 1948,
etc., i.e., every fourth year, the Presidential election is held.

November 11: Armistice Day, subsequently changed to
Veterans Day

Fourth Thursday in November: Thanksgiving Day

Following are the additional days citizens may display the flag:

January 1: New Year's Day

Easter Sunday (variable)

Third Saturday in May: Armed Forces Day

December 25: Christmas Day

Also on state holidays and as proclaimed by the President
of the United States

Rules for proper display of the flag:

In general, do not fly the flag at night. But when flying the flag
at night—at an athletic event, for example—properly light it.

To fold the flag, fold in half, width-wise, two times. Fold up a
triangle, starting at the striped end, then repeat until reaching
the end of the union (the field of stars) is exposed. Then fold
down the square into a triangle and tuck the folds inside.

When displaying the flag above a street, suspend it vertically,
with the Union to the north in an east and west street; to the east
in a north and south street.

Protect the flag in poor weather.

Do not place any object or emblem on or above the flag.

If a flag is in poor condition, it is preferable to destroy it by
burning it in a secluded area.

Never display an object on or above the flag itself, except when
using it as a statement of mourning.

When covering a casket, place the blue field over the left
shoulder of the deceased.

When displaying a flag on a pole, position the blue field at the
peak of the staff.

When displaying the U.S. flag with that of another nation,
always place the U.S. flag on the right as it faces observers.

When displaying a number of flags, on a stage, for example,
place the U.S. flag forward from the other and centered.

With a procession of flags, the U.S. flag is in the front of
the center line.

When displaying the flag vertically or horizontally on a wall,
place the blue field to the observers' left.

Do not use the flag as a covering on a ceiling.

Always carry the flag aloft, not flat—except in a situation
of distress.

Do not display the flag union down.

Never drape the flag itself. Instead, use red-white-and-blue
bunting.

Never use part of the flag for a costume or other garment.

To indicate mourning, fly the flag at half-mast. When this is not
possible, attach two black streamers to the spearhead.

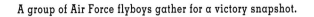

A group of Air Force flyboys gather for a victory snapshot.

"I was on the top of a hill fighting a fire and
heard horns honking and cannons going off . . .
there were fireworks and a lot of noise. It wasn't
until a day or so later that I learned the war was
over"—Norman Perry, Dallas, OR

Dated Events

Munich Agreement September 30, 1938
Russia signs Pact with Nazis August 23, 1939
Nazis invade Poland September 1, 1939
Great Britain, France, Australia, and New Zealand declare war on Nazis
    September 3, 1939
Canada declares war on Nazis September 10, 1939
Russia invades Finland November 30, 1939
Finland and Russia make peace March 12, 1940
Nazis invade Lowlands May 10, 1940
Italy declares war on Britain and France June 10, 1940
Russia secures rights in Lithuania June 15, 1940
Russian occupation of Latvia and Estonia June 16, 1940
Nazis dictate Armistice to France June 22, 1940
U.S.A. leases British bases for Joint Defense August 20, 1940
Italian Invasion of Egypt September 13, 1940
British offensive in Egypt December 9-10, 1940
British Army attacks Italian Somaliland Feb 11, 1941
Roosevelt signs Lend-Lease Bill March 11, 1941
Mogadiscio captured by British April 1, 1941
Nazis invade Greece and Yugoslavia April 6, 1941
Rommel invades Egypt April 14, 1941
H.M.S. Hood sunk May 24, 1941
Bismarck sunk May 27, 1941
Nazis invade Russia June 22, 1941
Roosevelt and Churchill arrange Atlantic Charter August 14, 1941
2nd British offensive in Egypt November 18, 1941
Canada declares war on Japan December 8, 1941
U.S. declares war on Germany and Italy December 11, 1941
First Americans arrive in Britain January 28, 1942
British occupy Madagascar May 6, 1942
Mexico declares war on Axis May 22, 1942
U.S. declares war on Bulgaria, Hungary, and Rumania June 5, 1942
Darian turns over Dakar to United Nations November 24, 1942
Roosevelt-Churchill Unconditional Surrender Conference
    January 14-24, 1943
Siege of Leningrad lifted January 18, 1943
Rommel driven from Libya February 10, 1943
Axis driven from Africa May 13, 1943
Allies invade Sicily July 9-10, 1943
Mussolini ousted July 25, 1943
Italy surrenders to Allies September 8, 1943
U.S. forces land on Salerno, Italy September 9, 1943

Iran declares war on Nazis September 9, 1943
Portugal grants Allies use of Azores October 12, 1943
Italy declares war on Germany October 13, 1943
U.S.-Russia-Great Britain Conference October 19-30, 1943
U.S.-Great Britain-China Conference November 22-26, 1943
Roosevelt-Stalin-Churchill, Tehran Conference
    November 28-December 1, 1943
Gen. Eisenhower made invasion leader December 24, 1943
Rome falls to Allies June 4, 1944
D-Day landings in Normandy June 6, 1944
Russia opens summer offensive on Finland June 9, 1944
Allies invade Southern France August 15, 1944
Dumbarton Oaks Conference August 21-October 7, 1944
Rumania joins Allies August 23, 1944
Paris liberated August 25, 1944
Soviet troops capture Bucharest August 31, 1944
Brussels liberated September 3, 1944
Finland signs Armistice September 5, 1944
Russia declares war on Bulgaria September 5, 1944
Bulgaria declares war on Germany September 8, 1944
Russia grants Bulgaria Armistice September 9, 1944
Yanks invade Germany September 11, 1944
Roosevelt and Churchill meet in Quebec September 11, 1944
Luxembourg liberated September 11, 1944
Russia and Rumania sign Armistice September 12, 1944
Russia and Finland sign Peace Agreement September 20, 1944
Allies invade Albania, Yugoslavia, and Greece September 27, 1944
Athens liberated October 14, 1944
Belgrade liberated October 20, 1944
Allies recognize De Gaulle regime October 23, 1944
Russia invades Norway October 25, 1944
British sink Tirpitz November 12, 1944
Tirana liberated November 18, 1944
Germany starts counter offensive December 16, 1944
Russia opens winter offensive January 12, 1945
Russia liberates Warsaw January 17, 1945
Roosevelt-Churchill and Stalin hold Crimea Conference
    February 4-11, 1945
Inter-American Conference February 21, 1945
Yanks cross Rhine March 7, 1945
Konigsberg falls to Russians April 6, 1945
President Roosevelt dies April 12, 1945
Russians capture Vienna April 13, 1945
Russians enter Berlin April 23, 1945

U.S. and Russian Armies meet on the Elbe April 25, 1945
Mussolini shot by Italian partisans April 28, 1945
Gen. Clark reports Italian Campaign over April 30, 1945
Hitler reported dead May 1, 1945
Germany signs unconditional surrender terms at Reims, France, witnessed
    by Big Three powers May 7, 1945
V-E day proclaimed by President Truman and Prime Minister Churchill
    May 8, 1945
Stalin announces surrender of Germany May 4, 1945
Unconditional surrender by Germany to Russia at Berlin May 8, 1945
Joachim Von Ribbentrop captured in Hamburg June 14, 1945
Announce meeting of Big Three in Berlin June 15, 1945
Gen. Eisenhower, allied supreme commander in Europe, returns to
    Washington June 18, 1945

Dated events, Pacific Area Theater

Japan makes war on China January 1932
Japan joins Axis September 27, 1940
Russian-Japanese non-aggression pact April 13, 1941
Vichy surrenders Indo China to Japs July 1941
Japanese attack Pearl Harbor December 7, 1941
Japan declares war on U.S. and Britain December 7, 1941
U.S. declares war on Japan December 8, 1941
Guam captures by Japanese December 13, 1941
Wake captured by Japanese December 24, 1941
Hong Kong captured by Japanese December 25, 1941
Singapore falls February 15, 1942
California Coast shelled by Japanese submarine February 23, 1942
Batavia falls to Japanese March 5, 1942
MacArthur takes command in the Southwest Pacific March 17, 1942
Rangoon falls to Japanese March 20, 1942
Bataan captured by Japanese April 9, 1942
1st United Nations Air Raid on Tokyo April 18, 1942
Corregidor captured by Japanese May 6, 1942
Japanese Navy defeated in Coral Sea May 7, 1942
Japanese bomb Dutch Harbor June 3, 1942
Japanese Navy defeated at Midway June 7, 1942
Japanese land on Aleutians June 12, 1942
U.S. Marines land on Solomon Islands August 7, 1942
Japanese defeated in Naval battles by U.S. August 8–November 13, 1942
U.S. lands on Attu May 11, 1943
Japanese Navy defeated in Kula Gulf July 13, 1943
Yanks take Munda August 5, 1943
Japanese cleaned out of Aleutians August 15, 1943
Mountbatten takes Allied Command in Burma August 16, 1943
Salamaua taken by Allies September 13, 1943
Lae taken by Allies September 16, 1943
Gilbert Island cleaned of Japanese November 20–23, 1943
U.S. invades New Britain December 25, 1943
Yanks land on Marshall Islands January 31, 1944
U.S. Navy raids Truk February 16–17, 1944

U.S. Navy raids Saipan February 22, 1944
U.S. invades Admiralty Islands March 1, 1944
Allied forces land at Hollandia April 22, 1944
U.S. invades Wakde May 17, 1944
U.S. invades Biak May 27, 1944
U.S. invades Saipan June 15, 1944
Japanese Premier Tojo and Cabinet resign July 18, 1944
U.S. invades Guam July 21, 1944
U.S. invades Tinian July 25, 1944
Roosevelt, MacArthur, and Nimitz meet at Hawaii July 29, 1944
Superforts bomb Nagasaki and Sumatra August 10, 1944
Japan bombed by B29s June 15, July 6, August 20, 1944
U.S. Navy attacks Philippines September 11-20-23, 1944
U.S. invades Halmaheras and Palau September 15, 1944
B24s bomb Borneo October 1–6, 1944
U.S. Navy strikes Marcus Islands October 8, 1944
U.S. Carrier Force and Superforts bomb Formosa October 11–14, 1944
U.S. invades Philippines Oct 17, 1944
Japanese Navy routed near Philippines October 23-30, 1944
B29s bomb Singapore and Sumatra November 5, 1944
B29s bomb Nanking and Shanghai November 11, 1944
First B29 raid from Saipan November 24, 1944
First B29 night raid on Japan November 29, 1944
U.S. invades Mindoro December 15, 1944
U.S. invades Luzon January 9, 1945
Manila liberated February 4, 1945
U.S. captures Bataan February 15, 1945
U.S. invades Corregidor February 16, 1945
U.S. invades Iwo Jima February 19, 1945
U.S. invades Palawan February 28, 1945
U.S. invades Mindanao March 8, 1945
Iwo Jima captured by American troops March 16, 1945
U.S. invades Ryukyu Island March 26, 1945
U.S. invades Tawitawi Islands and Masbate April 4, 1945
Russia denounces Neutrality Pact with Tokyo April 5, 1945
Premier Koiso Cabinet falls April 5, 1945
Photographer Ernie Pyle killed in Action April 17, 1945
San Francisco World Security Conference April 25, 1945
Australians land on Tarakan Island, Borneo May 1, 1945
Rangoon falls to British May 3, 1945
Superforts drop 3,000 tons of fire-bombs on Kobe June 6, 1945
Naha airfield captured June 7, 1945
Superforts raid Nagoya, Akashi on Honshu June 9, 1945
Australian troops land in Brunei Bay, Borneo June 10, 1945
U.S. 10th Army gains foothold on Yaeju S. Okinawa June 12, 1945
Chinese troops capture port of Wenchow, China June 18, 1945
Lt. Gen. Buckner, Jr., killed in action June 19, 1945
Okinawa captured by American troops June 22, 1945
Miri, Borneo, captured June 27, 1945
Australian troops land on Balikpapan, Borneo July 1, 1945
Gen. MacArthur announces liberation of the Philippines July 5, 1945